D1266025

J 363.2 A
VB
3/16

Highway Patrol Officers

by Miriam Aronin

Consultant: William D. Healy
Retired Ohio State Highway Patrol Staff Lieutenant
Director, North Coast Polytechnic Institute
North Ridgeville, Ohio

BEARPORT
PUBLISHING

New York, New York

Credits

Cover and Title Page, © Petr Student/Shutterstock, © John Roman Images/Shutterstock, © Bikeriderlondon/Shutterstock, © A.B.G./Shutterstock, and © Robynrg/Shutterstock; 4, © Mindy Linford/Dreamstime; 5T, © Glenn Moore/ZUMA Press/Newscom; 5B, © FA Jon/Wikimedia Commons; 6L, © Mikadun/Shutterstock; 6R, © Nutkamol komolvanich/Shutterstock; 7L, © Andreas Fuhrmann/ZUMA Press/Newscom; 7R, © Peter Armstrong/Dreamstime; 8, © Mark Duncan/AP/Corbis; 9, © Karl Mondon/ZUMA Press/Newscom; 10, © Peppenero/Dreamstime; 11, © Jakowski308/Dreamstime; 12, © Gabriele Tamborrelli/iStock; 13T, Courtesy the Ohio State Highway Patrol; 13B, Courtesy the Ohio State Highway Patrol; 14, © fabiodevilla/Shutterstock; 15T, Courtesy the Ohio State Highway Patrol; 15B, © michal812/Shutterstock; 16L, © Jose M. Osorio/Sacramento Bee/ZUMA Press/Newscom; 16B, © Jens Molin/Shutterstock; 17, Courtesy the Missouri State Highway Patrol; 18, © Gary Cosby Jr./Associated Press; 19L, © egdigital/iStock; 19TR, Courtesy the Missouri State Highway Patrol; 19BR, Courtesy the Missouri State Highway Patrol; 20–21, © J.B. Forbes/Associated Press; 21R, Courtesy the Missouri State Highway Patrol; 22, © amygdala_imagery/iStock; 23, © JohnPitcher/iStock; 24L, © Rich Pedroncelli/Associated Press; 24R, © CreativeHQ/Shutterstock; 25, © The (San Luis Obispo) Tribune/ZUMA Press/Newscom; 26T, © egd/Shutterstock; 26B, ksb/Shutterstock; 27, LUMIKK555/iStock; 28T, © Mountain Democrat/ZUMA Press/Newscom; 28B, © Gringos4/Dreamstime; 29TL, © ksb/Shutterstock; 29TR, © dcwcreations/Shutterstock; 29BL, © CPC Collection/Alamy Stock Photo; 29BM, © Andrey Nekrasov/imageBROKER; 29BR, © Image Point Fr/Shutterstock; 31, © Denise Kappa/Shutterstock.

Publisher: Kenn Goin
Senior Editor: Joyce Tavolacci
Creative Director: Spencer Brinker
Photo Researcher: We Research Pictures, LLC

Library of Congress Cataloging-in-Publication Data

Aronin, Miriam, author.
  Highway patrol officers / by Miriam Aronin.
    pages cm. — (Police: search & rescue!)
  Includes bibliographical references and index.
  ISBN 978-1-943553-14-3 (library binding) — ISBN 1-943553-14-9 (library binding)
  1. Motorcycle police—Juvenile literature 2. Traffic police—Juvenile literature. 3. Police patrol—Juvenile literature. I. Title.
  HV8020.A76 2016
  363.2'332—dc23

                            2015033094

For more information, write to Bearport Publishing Company, Inc., 45 West 21st Street, Suite 3B, New York, New York 10010. Printed in the United States of America.

10 9 8 7 6 5 4 3 2 1

Contents

A Serious Fall

On June 9, 2015, 17-year-old Andrew Musgrave was hiking with friends near a huge waterfall in California's Sierra Nevada Mountains. Suddenly, Andrew lost his balance and fell. His friends watched in horror as he tumbled 40 feet (12 m) down the steep waterfall and landed on a large rock. "He was kind of rolling down the cliff," said Nolan Hargaray-Conter, Andrew's friend.

Andrew and his friends were hiking near this waterfall, called Horsetail Falls, when he fell.

Andrew's friends rushed down the mountain to the spot where Andrew had fallen and called for help. It was clear that their friend had broken bones and needed help **urgently**. The California Highway Patrol (CHP) answered the call and quickly **dispatched** a rescue helicopter to the scene. Would help arrive in time to save Andrew's life?

A CHP rescue helicopter

Helicopters are often used to search for and rescue people in the mountains.

A Daring Rescue

Not long after their call for help, Andrew's friends heard the loud whirring sound of a helicopter above them. The spot where Andrew had fallen was too steep for the **chopper** to land, so the helicopter **crew** used a cable to lower an officer to the ground. Then the crew prepared a hoist to rescue Andrew.

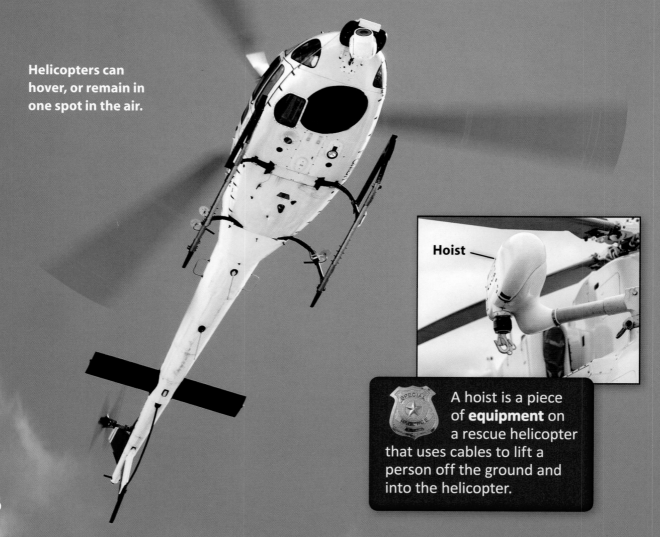

Helicopters can hover, or remain in one spot in the air.

Hoist

A hoist is a piece of **equipment** on a rescue helicopter that uses cables to lift a person off the ground and into the helicopter.

6

As the chopper hovered in the air, one of the crew members lowered a large carrier called a Stokes basket to the officer on the ground. The officer carefully loaded Andrew into the basket and wrapped four strong straps around him. The straps connected to more than 100 feet (30 m) of cables. Andrew was then lifted up to the chopper and flown to a nearby hospital. The CHP had saved the teen's life. "They put themselves at risk to get in there and save him," said Andrew's grateful mother.

The CHP rescues a person in the mountains using a hoist and Stokes basket.

Stokes basket

A Stokes basket is also called a litter.

Meet the Highway Patrol

The highway patrol is a special police unit usually in charge of road safety. Nineteen U.S. states have a highway patrol. The other states, except for Hawaii, have a state police or a state patrol division. Highway patrol officers make sure people wear seat belts and drive safely. They also help rescue people from accidents on state roads and highways.

Highway patrol members are called officers or troopers.

Yet many highway patrol units deal with far more than just roads and cars. In California, the highway patrol is the main police group in the state. One of the CHP's most important jobs is to help save lives during **emergencies** and **disasters**. It searches for and rescues people who are lost or hurt on mountains, in forests, in floodwaters—or in any other hard-to-reach places.

Both men and women work as officers for the CHP.

California has the largest highway patrol of any state. In 2013, it had more than 10,000 officers.

Rescue Choppers

To carry out search and rescue **missions**, highway patrol officers use many kinds of equipment. One of the most important tools they use is the helicopter. Choppers can get to areas that are difficult to access by foot or by car. These machines can also move quickly—up to 145 miles per hour (233 kph)!

The inside of a highway patrol rescue helicopter is often filled with emergency medical equipment and looks like a small ambulance.

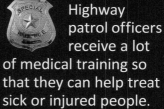

Highway patrol officers receive a lot of medical training so that they can help treat sick or injured people.

Most rescue helicopters carry at least three crewmembers: a pilot, a flight officer, and a hoist operator. All of the team members work together during a rescue. The pilot keeps the helicopter steady, while the hoist operator lowers the flight officer and Stokes basket down to the ground with a cable. Once the officer is on the ground and has loaded the person being rescued into the Stokes basket, the team winds up the cables to lift the person and the officer up. "It's a high-stress **environment**," says pilot Joe Kingman. If the cable gets tangled, it may put the person being rescued in danger. "There's no room for confusion."

skids

An officer sits or stands on the landing skids of the chopper to operate the hoist. To keep from falling, he or she wears a special harness that's attached to the inside of the helicopter.

Auto Emergency

Not all highway patrol rescuers use helicopters. Officers also use police cars to race to rescues. On the morning of December 8, 2008, Deborah and James Berry were driving in Medina, Ohio. Without warning, another car turned sharply in front of their car. The Berrys' vehicle crashed into the other car and then slammed into a metal **guardrail**.

Despite being shaken from the accident, James managed to call 9-1-1 for help. Two Ohio State Highway Patrol (OSHP) officers rushed to the accident. When they arrived, Sergeant Matthew Witmer smelled smoke. Trooper Bryan Foxx spotted a flame under the car's hood. They knew they had to act fast to save the couple inside the crumpled vehicle before it exploded.

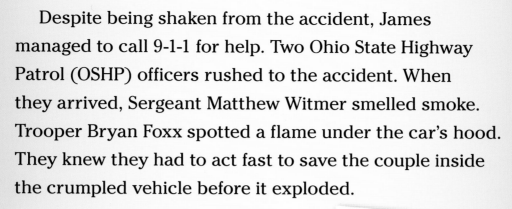

In 2014, more than 100,000 people were injured in car crashes in Ohio.

OSHP Sergeant
Matthew Witmer

OSHP Trooper
Bryan Foxx

Real-Life Heroes

Trooper Foxx grabbed a **fire extinguisher** from the police car and began battling the growing blaze. James managed to climb out of the car, but Deborah's hip and leg were badly broken and she couldn't move. "We focused on the fact that we had to get her out," said Sergeant Witmer. Without hesitation, he crawled into the blazing car. With James's help, Sergeant Witmer was able to carefully pull Deborah to safety. A moment later, they felt a rush of heat. The whole car burst into flames.

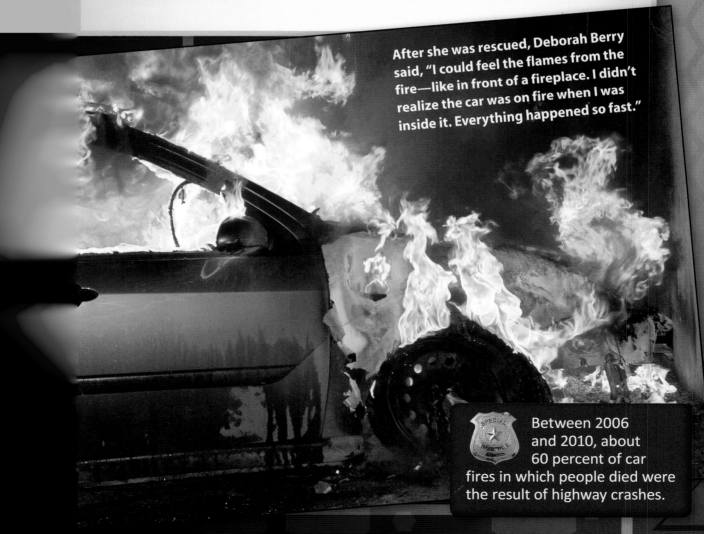

After she was rescued, Deborah Berry said, "I could feel the flames from the fire—like in front of a fireplace. I didn't realize the car was on fire when I was inside it. Everything happened so fast."

Between 2006 and 2010, about 60 percent of car fires in which people died were the result of highway crashes.

On February 6, 2009, Sergeant Witmer and Trooper Foxx received the OSHP's highest honor—an award called the Citation of Merit. At the ceremony, Highway Patrol Colonel Richard H. Collins praised the men for risking their own lives to save Deborah.

Sergeant Witmer (center) and Trooper Foxx (right) were recognized by Colonel Collins (left) and the state of Ohio for their heroic rescue of Deborah Berry.

Training Hard

It takes special training to prepare for a fiery rescue or other emergency. Highway patrol officers learn many of the skills they need at the **police academy**. At the California Highway Patrol Academy in Sacramento, **cadets** receive more than 1,100 hours of training. "They train hard," explains CHP Officer Steve Tanguay. The cadets take classes in **self-defense** and other skills. They also participate in **grueling** workouts to keep their bodies strong.

Captain Cathy A. Sulinski at the entrance to the CHP Academy

Many highway patrol cadets learn how to perform **CPR** and other life-saving skills.

Some highway patrol officers get extra search and rescue training in the water. Members of the Missouri State Highway Patrol (MSHP) learn how to become expert **scuba** divers and get five weeks of underwater training. They also become skilled at rescuing people who are at risk of drowning or are victims of boating accidents.

MSHP Dive Team members learn to rescue people in raging rivers.

Flood

Highway patrol officers are used to facing danger on the job. On April 18, 2013, heavy rain was falling in Douglas County, Missouri. At 8:10 A.M., the MSHP received a call. An elderly couple reported that water from an overflowing creek had surrounded their mobile home and was quickly pouring inside. The couple was trapped. How would they get out?

A flooded mobile home

Luckily, MSHP Troopers Daniel J. Johnson and Jason W. Philpott were close by. They parked their patrol car in a field near the mobile home and used an **inflatable** rescue boat to reach the house. When the troopers got to the front door, Trooper Johnson stepped into the house and put life jackets on the frightened couple. Then he carefully helped them into the boat.

Trooper Daniel J. Johnson

Trooper Jason W. Philpott

Highway patrol officers often use small, air-filled rafts or larger patrol boats (above) to rescue people from floods.

Swept Away

As the troopers tried to pull away from the mobile home, the boat's motor got tangled in wire. The small boat was turned sideways by the creek's strong **current**. Water began to gush inside. The troopers tried to paddle to safety, but it was too late. The boat had begun to sink with the troopers and elderly couple inside!

Even a small amount of floodwater can be dangerous. Just 1 foot (0.3 m) of flowing water can sweep away a car.

The rushing water then swept the two troopers and the couple out of the boat and into the creek. They were carried toward a nearby concrete bridge by the fast-moving water. If the troopers didn't act fast, they would all crash into the base of the bridge. The troopers grabbed hold of the couple. Then they swam against the current with all their strength. Finally, they made it to a small patch of land. At last, they were safe!

Troopers Johnson and Philpott received the Missouri Medal of Valor for their bravery during the water rescue.

Stalked!

Every highway patrol rescue is different, and some are more unusual than others. Late in the afternoon on February 16, 2013, the CHP got a strange call. David Nash was hiking on a mountain pass called Stevens Trail in California when he realized he was being **stalked** . . . by a huge mountain lion! David tried to scare away the big cat. He blew a loud whistle and shined a flashlight at it. Yet nothing worked.

A hiker in the California mountains

For about an hour, the huge cat kept circling David. It crept closer and closer. When it was only 25 feet (7.6 m) away, David became afraid it was getting ready to attack. He used his phone to call for help. Luckily, a CHP helicopter was already in the area.

Most mountain lions do not attack humans.

If a mountain lion is nearby, do not run. If you run, it might chase after you.

To the Rescue

Officers Monty Emery and David White headed to Stevens Trail in their chopper. By then, it was getting dark. The officers had to use **night-vision goggles** to find David. They quickly spotted him and the mountain lion.

Some night-vision goggles use thermal imaging. Thermal imaging shows the heat people and animals give off. This helps rescuers find people and animals in the dark.

Night-vision goggles

CHP Officers Emery and White flew to the area where David was being stalked.

The officers looked for a safe place to land but couldn't find one. They decided to fly the noisy chopper as close to the mountain lion as they could. Their plan worked! The chopper's loud spinning **rotor blades** frightened the big cat. It took off and ran up the mountain. "I'd never scared off a mountain lion before using a helicopter," said Officer Emery.

Officers Emery and White used a helicopter like this one to scare away the mountain lion.

Saving Lives

Not all highway patrol rescues involve saving people. On May 9, 2014, the CHP got an emergency call about an animal stuck on a busy highway. Officer Alex Edmon hopped on his CHP motorcycle and hurried to the freeway to help. When he arrived, he found a tiny Chihuahua! She was lying on the concrete divider in the center of the road. Traffic whizzed by her on either side as he rushed to help her.

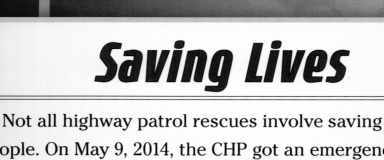

The little dog was very frightened. Officer Edmon petted her and offered her food. He kept her safe until **animal control** officers could get her. Many people heard about the amazing rescue, which became a national news story. In response to all the attention, the highway patrol said simply, "We're big on saving lives."

 Officer Edmon named the Chihuahua "Freeway."

Chihuahuas are very small, often weighing no more than 6 pounds (2.7 kg).

Highway Patrol Officers' Equipment

Highway patrol officers use special equipment. Here is some of their gear.

Highway patrol helicopters use hoists to rescue people from hard-to-reach places.

A *hoist*

When an injured person is carried in a Stokes basket, a *Bauman Bag* is used to keep him or her safe.

Highway patrol cars carry lots of gear, including fire extinguishers to help put out fires.

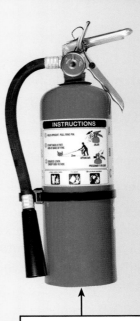

A *fire extinguisher*

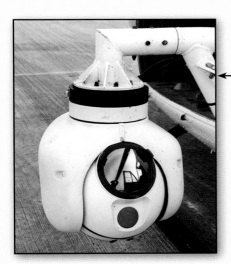

Highway patrol helicopters and airplanes use *FLIR infrared cameras* to find people in the dark. Pictures from these cameras show warm areas, such as humans and animals, in bright white.

Underwater metal detectors are used to help search for lost objects underwater.

Glossary

animal control (AN-uh-muhl kuhn-TROHL) an organization in charge of carrying out laws related to animals

cadets (kah-DEHTS) people in training to be highway patrol officers or troopers

chopper (CHOP-uhr) a helicopter

CPR (SEE-PEA-AR) *CPR* stands for cardiopulmonary resuscitation; a type of rescue where a person blows air into the mouth and then presses down on the chest of someone whose heart has stopped

crew (KROO) a group of people who work together

current (KUR-uhnt) the movement of water in an ocean, river, or flood

disasters (duh-ZAHS-turz) events that cause terrible destruction

dispatched (dihs-PACHD) sent people out, usually in vehicles, to assist others

emergencies (ih-MUR-juhn-seez) sudden situations that must be dealt with immediately

environment (en-VYE-ruhn-muhnt) a certain place or situation

equipment (i-KWIP-muhnt) the tools or machines needed to do a job

fire extinguisher (FIRE ehk-STIHN-gwish-ur) something used to put out a fire, often using chemicals

guardrail (GARD-rayl) a metal bar or fence that stops cars from driving off the road

grueling (GROO-uh-ling) very hard, difficult, or tiring

inflatable (in-FLAY-tuh-buhl) able to be blown up with air

missions (MISH-uhnz) special jobs

night-vision goggles (NITE-VIHZH-uhn GAH-guhlz) a device that people can look through to see clearly in the dark

police academy (puh-LEES uh-KAD-uh-mee) a school that trains students to become police officers

rotor blades (ROH-tur BLAYDZ) the parts of the helicopter that turn and lift the helicopter into the air

scuba (SKOO-buh) diving equipment that lets a person breathe under the water; *scuba* stands for *self-contained underwater breathing apparatus*

self-defense (SELF-dee-FEHNTS) skills to protect oneself during an attack

stalked (STAWKD) hunted

urgently (UR-juhnt-lee) quickly or immediately

Bibliography

DeVroede, Tera. "The CHP Academy Offers an Inside Look at Training, Preparing Officers," *Lake County News* (April 24, 2010).

Phelps, Mark. "Helicopter Rescues Hiker from Mountain Lion," *Flying* (February 22, 2013).

Sherburne, Creig P. "CHP Is Not AAA with a Badge," *Atascadero News* (October 7, 2011).

Witmer, Sgt. Matthew, and Deborah Berry. "Surviving a Fiery Car Crash," *Cleveland Magazine* (May 2009).

Read More

Blake, Kevin. *Air-Sea Rescue Officers (Police: Search & Rescue!)*. New York: Bearport (2016).

Ollhoff, Jim. *Search & Rescue (Emergency Workers)*. Minneapolis, MN: ABDO (2013).

Randolph, Joanne. *Emergency Helicopters (To the Rescue!)*. New York: PowerKids Press (2008).

Learn More Online

To learn more about highway patrol officers, visit
www.bearportpublishing.com/PoliceSearchAndRescue

Index

About the Author

Miriam Aronin is a writer and editor living in Chicago, Illinois. She enjoys reading, knitting, baking, and learning about new topics—like the highway patrol!